Verses of a Lowly Fakir

MADHO LAL HUSSEIN

Translated from the Punjabi by Naveed Alam

PENGUIN BOOKS

An imprint of Penguin Random House

PENGUIN BOOKS

USA | Canada | UK | Ireland | Australia
New Zealand | India | South Africa | China | Singapore

Penguin Books is part of the Penguin Random House group of companies
whose addresses can be found at global.penguinrandomhouse.com

Published by Penguin Random House India Pvt. Ltd
4th Floor, Capital Tower 1, MG Road,
Gurugram 122 002, Haryana, India

First published by Penguin Books India 2016

Translation copyright © Naveed Alam 2016

10 9 8 7 6 5 4 3 2

ISBN 9780670088270

Typeset in Bembo Std by Manipal Digital Systems, Manipal
Printed at Replika Press Pvt. Ltd, India

www.penguin.co.in

This is a legitimate digitally printed version of the book and therefore might not
have certain extra finishing on the cover.

For Sa'ad, my Madho, my Lal

Contents

Acknowledgements

Grateful acknowledgement is made to the editors of the following journals who first published versions of the kafis: *The Adirondack Review* (kafis 3, 10, 25, 47, 48), *International Poetry Review* (kafis 49, 61, 63, 65, 66), *91st Meridian* (kafis 37, 16, 21, 146), *Metamorphoses* (kafis 136, 52, 54, 56, 69, 70) and *Papercuts* (kafi 43).

I am truly grateful to Ambar Sahil Chatterjee, my editor at Penguin, for all his help and tireless support. Mriga Maithel, my copy editor, deserves the kudos for shaping the manuscript. Many thanks to R. Sivapriya for helping add Madho Lal Hussein to the Penguin Classics list. Thanks to Bilal Tanweer for directing me across the border for a publisher.

I might not have taken up this project if it hadn't been for Ida Sofie Matzen who took me along to the shrines in Lahore while doing her doctoral research. *Tak*, Ida, for the spark. Thank you, Spring Ulmer, for being such a generous reader and insightful commentator. Sa'ad Baqar, I can't thank you enough for being who you are. And my eternal gratitude to the singers—well-known artists as well as lesser-known minstrels—whose voices led me to Shah Hussein's poetry.

The Disgraceful Saint
An Introduction

The portrait of Shah Hussein (1538–99), popularly known as Madho Lal Hussein, that emerges after piecing together the details of his life based on traditional sources, makes him out to be a Punjabi Dionysus: drunkenly he roams the streets of Lahore in the company of fellow carousers, breaks off the chains when officials approach to arrest him, baffles Akbar, the reigning emperor of the time, by appearing in his private chambers when he's supposed to be locked up, and turns wine into water, sherbet, milk, tea, vinegar and back to wine again.

Weaver, mystic, fakir, Shah Hussein continues to command great reverence in Punjab as a poet–saint more than 400 years after his death. His *urs*, or death anniversary, is still celebrated at his shrine in Baghbanpura, Lahore. In the inner sanctum of the shrine, buried right next to Hussein, is his young beloved and disciple, Madho (pronounced *Madh-oh*) Lal. The fact that Hussein literally fused his name with Madho's and came to be known as Madho Lal Hussein is not only testament to the enduring legacy of love, but also illustrates an essential tenet of Sufism, the merger of the lover and the beloved. This work

xi

of translation uses Hussein's self-given name in the title as homage to the poet's queer passion.

To understand the subversive wisdom of Hussein's *kafis* (singular *kafi*, the stanza-length poetic form preferred by most Punjabi and Sindhi mystical poets) and his unconventional lifestyle practised in sixteenth-century Punjab, we must delve into the scant biographical sources available.

Hussein's father, a Rajput from the Kalsrai clan, converted to Islam during the Delhi Sultanate (1206–1526) and took on the Muslim name of Sheikh Usman. As a boy, Hussein joined the local mosque which also functioned as a madrasa, where memorizing the Quran by rote was the main method of learning. Being a prodigious student, Hussein caught the attention of an itinerant dervish and scholar, Sheikh Bahlol Dariai, who took him under his wing. The Sheikh was a learned man, having travelled across the wide expanse of the fifteenth-century Islamic world, including Arabia, Mesopotamia, Persia and Afghanistan. He broadened the parochial horizons of his young ward, daring Hussein to fathom the unconventional ways in which traditional texts could be interpreted.

Later, at the age of thirty-six, while studying with another respected scholar of the time, Sheikh Sa'ad Ullah, Hussein paused at the following verses from the Quran:

Harken, Ye Folks, the world is a play and a show, a display of pageantry, pride, and boasting between yourselves, and competing with one another for greater wealth and number of children.

(Sura Al-Hadid 57: 20)

The words resonated so deeply with Hussein that he broke into a spontaneous dance of self-liberation. From this point onwards, he would not play the game for the sake of any success in the world, material or spiritual, but would rather become the amused player who treats the world as what it is: an ephemeral playground.

It was only a matter of time before Sheikh Bahlol Dariai heard of the promising young student turned *malamati*—one who seeks disgrace and censure—leading his pack of revellers through the town. The Sheikh returned to talk some sense into Hussein, and he received his due reverence despite Hussein's radically altered lifestyle. When asked to lead the prayers, Hussein complied. In the middle of the prayer, Hussein broke into laughter and ran away when he recited these Quranic verses:

Did We not open your heart, and ease your burden which weighed down your back, and exalted your fame?

(Sura Ash-Sharh 94:1–4)

In time, Hussein acquired quite a reputation: a rebel fakir dressed in all red, bearing a wine flask in one hand and an earthen bowl in another. This popular figure did not make for an exemplary model to enforce the moral codes based on the puritanical values of the religious elite. And yet the swelling numbers of his followers could not have gone unchecked since Akbar had temporarily shifted his capital to Lahore. According to legend, the emperor was unimpressed by the wine-to-non-alcoholic-drinks miracle performed by Hussein when he was brought before Akbar for interrogation, and sent him to prison. While Hussein was in the dock, his likeness showed up in the harem attended upon by the royal ladies. Mystified by the miraculous feat, Akbar acknowledged Hussein's credentials as a saint, and set him free.[1]

There is no account of Hussein in the annals of Akbar, though the Mughals were known for their meticulous record-keeping. Jehangir, Akbar's successor, is supposed to have appointed a person by the name of Bahar Khan to keep a daily log of Hussein's activities and sayings. No copy of his work, *Baharia*, is extant. Noor Ahmed Chisti makes an unverifiable claim to have consulted it, but the book remains the Holy Grail for Shah Hussein's modern historians. No mention of Hussein is made even in *Tuzk-i-Jehangiri*,[2] Jehangir's official memoir. According to Muhammad Asif Khan, only Dara Shikoh—Shah Jahan's heir apparent who lost the battle of succession to his brother, Aurangzeb—mentions Hussein twice in his work, *Hasnat al-Arafeen*.[3] He calls him Hussein Dadha, using Hussein's matrilineal family name (his mother belonged to the Dadha clan of Rajputs).

Haqiqat al-Fuqra (*Truth of the Saints*), written around 1660 by Sheikh Mahmud, commonly known as Muhammad Pir, established the trend for hagiography that continues till the present.[4] Another oft-cited source is the *Tehqiqat-i-Chisti: Tarikh-i-Lahore ka Encyclopedia* (*Researches of Chisti: Encyclopedia of Lahore's History*) by Noor Ahmed Chisti.[5] The latter heavily relies on the former. Despite their hagiographic tendencies, both authors help draw a tentative sketch of Hussein.

What's conspicuously missing from all the above sources is any reference to Shah Hussein's poetry. Muhammad Pir and Noor Ahmed Chisti are not concerned with Hussein, the poet, or Hussein, the self-proclaimed weaver, but remain fixated on Hussein, the saint. This is quite in contrast with how Hussein signs off at the end of almost every kafi: *fakir nimana* (the lowly fakir). Both men are unabashedly partial to Islam—for instance, Hussein's young lover's subsequent conversion to Islam is treated as a necessary step towards the latter's salvation, whereas Hussein's participation in the Hindu festival of Holi fails to draw the authors' attention towards the spiritual syncretism of the lover and the beloved. Both writers seem bent upon justifying the blatantly heterodox lifestyle of Hussein, especially his state of perpetual inebriation, as the prescribed norm of a *malamati* mystic. Could it be possible that the saint was much more palatable for the established elites, religious and political, than the rabble-rouser poet–weaver? Reverence, after all, lends itself to uncritical obeisance, but poetry is a powder keg, especially if the unschooled populace starts to quote it against the diktats of the sociopolitical order.

Passion and Devotion

Interestingly, the reverential texts do not refrain from dealing with some of the details of the relationship between Hussein and Madho Lal. This is how Muhammad Pir describes the love at first sight:

Madho was very beautiful and eccentrically proud. He was a Brahmin's son. Such a vain aesthete, vanity and pride apparent in his tipsy eyes. He was a Hindu, an infidel, a playful teaser, and cold-hearted. He was a torturer. He was known for flirting. From head to toe he was self-pride. On the way Hussein stood drunk. His friends were there as well. When he looked at Madho he sighed painfully and said: 'Friends, take heed. This boy has set my heart out of control. With one look he has made my heart restless. With one look he has taken away my heart. Taken the life out of my heart, and the soul out of my body. What should I do, friends? What should I do to make him fall in love? Friends, I've become a prisoner of his love. I shall not find peace till I see him.'[6]

Hussein keeps circling Madho's neighbourhood even after the proud young man spurns his advances. He persists, and demonstrates his mystical prowess by hearing what Madho says within the walls of his house and repeating the words verbatim. Finally, the youth yields and becomes a lover and devotee. It's the latter role that is emphasized in the traditional texts, though glimpses of something deeper than a platonic bond can be caught in the details meant to do just the opposite. For instance, when a follower of Hussein tries to spy on the two to satisfy his curiosity, he finds:

You [Hussein] are taking a glass of wine from Madho and kissing Madho on the forehead, and Madho is also kissing Hussein's forehead . . . Madho again gives a full glass to Shah Hussein, stands, and greets him respectfully.

Hussein also gets up and greets Madho respectfully. The two friends remained busy in this manner, and kept kissing each other like milk and sugar . . . and then the two friends became one.[7]

When the voyeur divulges the details to other men of Hussein's company, he is rebuked for not respecting a friend's privacy. The drunken kissing is explained as a propitious state of ecstasy for the transfer of mystical knowledge from a master to a disciple. The peeping Tom is told to go back and verify the truth. He returns and finds two terrifying lions sitting face-to-face.

For many a modern historian, the sainthood of Hussein has precluded the possibilities of exploring the nature of his relationship with Madho. The sexuality is either ignored, or downplayed, or dismissed outrightly: '[A] Sufi saint like Shah Hussain, why should he bother to adore an ordinary boy who had no spiritual background?' asks N. Hanif.[8] Another modern scholar, Dr Syed Nazir Ahmed, calculates the thirty-eight-year age gap between the two and concludes: '[W]ith such a difference of age even the possibility of a romantic relationship between them is repulsive to the mild taste.'[9] The scholars' reaction is quite indicative of the success of Hussein's avowed intentions: *tear up the ledger of saintly business* (kafi 99)—achieve self-degradation, especially in the eyes of the learned and the powerful. For a *malamati*, the ignominy ensures the grace. Something similar was practised by Divine, the drag queen protagonist of Jean Genet's *Our Lady of the Flowers*: 'I have placed myself lower than dirt. I could not do otherwise. If I declare that I am an old whore, no one can better that, I discourage insult. People can't even spit in my face any more.'[10]

There's no overt homosexuality in Hussein's work. Madho is addressed directly in only one kafi (kafi 21), and even there it's open to interpretation since the word 'Lal' can also mean dear or precious one. Ditto for kafi 102 where Hussein mentions Lal in the penultimate line (*Haven't found Lal yet*). Considering the speedy posthumous canonization of Hussein and the prevalence of the oral tradition, one has reason to speculate that some sort of character sanitization was at work. The likelihood of kafis with the 'objectionable' content being censored or suppressed cannot be ruled out. In this regard, it's important to note that no one denies Hussein's preference for the forbidden alcohol, yet there is no mention of wine, a common symbol of divine ecstasy in Persian mystical poetry, in any of the kafis. Kafi 147 with details of bhang-making stands out as the only outré kafi when it comes to intoxicants.

Only the Inflamed: The Use of the Female Voice

Hussein's *malamati*-style self-humiliation reaches its apogee in the line: *I'm the bitch at your doorstep* (kafi 5). His exultation in a disgraceful state is accentuated by the feminine noun. Imagine if he'd said, 'I'm the dog at your doorstep.' The feminization lends poignancy to the suffering, and explains why the narrator of the kafis is invariably female.

God, as in most religious traditions, is portrayed as male in Sufi poetry. The *urs* of a saint is celebrated as a wedding, the union of the bride/mortal with the groom/divine. While making mystical allusions, Hussein's female narrator often addresses fellow girlfriends, and worries about dowry (the deeds of mortal life) and the imminent departure from the parental home (leaving behind the comforts and attachments of the world) to join the husband's family, a foreign household of in-laws (afterlife).

Besides the conventional symbolism, the choice of assuming the female persona allows the poet to manipulate the tonal varieties of despair, a common device in the devotional poetry of South Asia. Radha must compete with the *gopi*s for Krishna's affections; only Sita bears the travails of *agni pariksha* (The Test of Fire). *Only the inflamed knows the flame. The rest is idle chatter* (kafis 9, 138). She suffers, for she's the embodiment of *prem* or devotion, and subsequently provides the poet with an inexhaustible reservoir of emotional intensity. Heer pines for Ranjha to the extent she loses her individual self:

> *I cried out my lover's name so often*
> *I turned into Ranjha myself*
> *Call me Ranjha, no one call me Heer*

(kafi 126)

By illustrating the indistinguishable merger of two individuals from the female perspective, the poet raises the anguish of separation a few notches—Heer challenges the codes of modesty by daring to say out loud the name of her lover, a lowly cowherd, to the point of assuming his given name. The references to Kheras (the family of social equals Heer is forced to marry into) in many of the kafis highlights the helplessness as well as defiance of the bride in a culture where arranged marriage is the norm and the woman's assent is taken for granted:

> *Mother, change if you can*
> *the course of my fate*
> *In a bridal palanquin*
> *Kheras carry me away*
> *I'm weak, I'm helpless*
> *Ranjha hooked me*
> *set storms in my heart*
> *The Almighty holds the string*
> *I squirm like a fish*
> *Says Hussein, the Master's fakir,*
> *False is the strength of Kheras*

(kafi 76)

Such explicit passion seals her fate, but it also gives the poet the opportunity to tweak the tropes of tragedy, polish the defiant note and amplify the decibels of plangent music.

'Indo-Muslim folk tradition has developed another peculiar facet under the influence of Hindu neighbors— the symbol of the woman soul,' says Annemarie Schimmel, an eminent Islamic scholar. Schimmel also points out that classical Sufism always interpreted *nafs* or the lower soul as female. A Sufi starts with *nafs ammara*, the basest level of selfish ego, and progresses to *nafs mutma 'inna*, the contented self.[11] Death before dying, a common refrain in Hussein's kafis, could be seen as the struggle between the higher and lower souls.

Hussein's kafis pull you into the world of a naïve weaver girl, an ingénue, a debutante, a hussy. She is either spinning away her days to prepare for a proper trousseau (aspiring for the *nafs mutma 'inna*), or avoiding the loom, sashaying around, splashing in the monsoon, wasting her time caught up in fun 'n' play (*nafs ammara*). Only the skilful bride is likely to embrace her groom, though the nature of the required skill is not too certain. The poor spinner may remain a spinster, for she was too engrossed in her chores. On the other hand, the one who burnt the veil and danced unabashedly may find the beau (kafi 101). *Bad, bad, bad, we're bad, folks. / Avoid us, the ill-reputed* (kafi 106).

The Weaver–Poet

Being a weaver–poet, Hussein's work is replete with references to the loom, spindle, thread and colour dyes. The latter, for instance, could be understood as a metaphor for the dissolution of ego into the colour of the beloved, the colour of passion: *lal* (red).

My colourful spinning wheel I painted red

(kafi 2)

I'm dyed in my Master's colours

(kafi 63)

In fact, the whole business of weaving is allegorical for the thread-by-thread disentanglement of the self in order to be rewoven into the pattern of the beloved:

You the warp, the weft, my each and everything is you
Says Hussein, the worthless fakir, I am nothing, You are all

(kafi 1)

or an invitation to step up to the task:

The path of love is a needle's eye
Be a thread, go through

(kafi 11)

The loom, a common household item, often appears in Punjabi folk songs. In Hussein's kafis, it functions almost like a prayer wheel:

In the rhythm of the circling loom
hear the call and the answer

(kafi 42)

Hussein's assertive self-identification as a weaver complicates the run-of-the-mill Sufi interpretation of his work. 'The poet's concern with the ultimate and eternal is not an indulgence in abstract speculation,' says Najm Hosain Syed, a contemporary Punjabi poet and a key figure in the renaissance of Shah Hussein.[12] Syed believes: 'It is a search for perspective to interpret everyday experience . . . a concern with the temporal and transient . . . an affirmation of the fact that he is intensely alive to the urgency and seriousness of the questions of this life.'[13]

What were the serious and urgent questions of Shah Hussein's times? A cursory search into the socio-economic conditions of Hussein's time yields W.H. Moreland's account of the so-called Golden Age of the Mughal rule.

> Weavers, naked themselves, toiled to clothe others. Peasants, themselves hungry, toiled to feed the towns and cities. India taken as a unit, parted with the useful commodities in exchange for gold and silver or in other words, gave bread for stones. . . . The only way to escape from the system lay through an increase in production, coupled with a rising standard of life, but this road was banned effectively by the administrative methods in vogue which penalized production of increased consumption as a signal for fresh extortion.[14]

Let's assume Moreland is just another imperial historian glorifying the British Raj at the expense of the brutal Mughal rule. However, there's the relevant historical account of a rebellion brewing in Punjab led by Abdullah Bhatti, commonly known as 'Dullah Bhatti, who was captured and hanged in public on Akbar's orders. In his play, *Takht L'hore* (*Throne of Lahore*), Najm Hosain Syed extrapolates the socio-economic conditions of Punjab, not different from the ones cited in Moreland's quote above.[15] Shah Hussein's character appears as a student of Sheikh Sa'ad Ullah and the son of a government contractor whose weaving factory has become a hotbed of 'Dullah sympathizers. Hussein's lyrical dialogues raise the suspicions of authorities, and towards the end of the play he's accused of riling the crowd outside the courthouse while the conspirators' trial is in session. As a historical figure, could Hussein, as Syed nudges us to think, be playing the true role of a fakir—the malcontent, the rebel, the subversive, the saboteur? Even hagiographers like Muhammad Pir and Chisti admit that Hussein kept eluding Akbar's police till he was finally nabbed at the hanging of 'Dullah Bhatti, though they make it sound as if he was attending the event as a mere spectator.

Most Punjabi Sufi poets were highly learned men, but they looked askance at scholars. Scholarly learning generally qualified one for self-enhancement rather than the Sufi goal of self-negation.

> *You read and read, became a learned scholar, a seeker of gold*
> *One hundred thousand books you read, but the cruel self*
> > *didn't die*
> *Without dispossession no one killed the thief within*
> > > > (Sultan Bahu, 1629–90)[16]

> *Enough of learning, my friend*
> *Only one letter 'A' is all you need*
> > > > (Bulleh Shah, 1680–1758)[17]

> *Outwardly pious, sordid within*
> *What a great man of learning you make*
> > > > > (kafi 11)

This streak of anti-intellectualism explains why Hussein chose Punjabi or the vernacular over Persian despite his erudition. Evidently, he was steering clear of the royal patronage and emoluments ensured through the use of court language. Ironically, his earliest full-length biography, *Haqiqat al-Fuqra*, is composed in Persian verse.

Kafi: A Poem and Song

Apart from the choice of the commoner's language and idiom, Hussein's use of the poetic form of kafi further illustrates his audience and intentions. Kafis, the stanzaic poems couched in folkloric themes and techniques, were easy to understand and memorize, and thus served as the ideal means to disseminate the mystical teachings among the illiterate masses dependent on the oral transmission of knowledge. Even to this day, most Punjabis and Sindhis are more likely to have heard a kafi than read one. The performative aspect of kafi can't be overemphasized. No matter how good a translator, the difference between reading a kafi and listening to it is similar to reading a play and watching it performed.

The origins of the word kafi have been traced to various sources: the Sanskrit words *kav* (poetry) and *kama* (sensuality), and the Arabic words *kamil* (perfection) and *kafa* (grouping). It's quite possible that the word may be rooted in the pre-Islamic literary tradition but later Islamized, as is the case with the origins of the Urdu language in the Indian subcontinent. Muhammad Asif Khan has tried to establish it as a sub-genre of Indian classical music in his

'What Is Kafi?', an introductory essay to Hussein's work that he edited.[18]

The first line of a kafi functions as a refrain, called *rahau* in Punjabi, and it's often repeated after every verse while the kafi is being sung. There is no consistent rhyming scheme. In some kafis, the last word of each line rhymes; in others, there could be a pattern of *a bb a bb a* or *aba aca ada*. In almost every concluding line, Hussein addresses himself as *fakir nimana* (the lowly fakir) or *fakir Sain da* (the Lord's fakir). Such a self-reference at the end of the poem contextualizes the warning or rebuke or lament or advice expressed earlier in the verse; in doing so, it levels the moral ground between the reader/listener and the poet/singer.

A kafi is meant to be a conversation between the disciple (*murid*) and the master (*murshid*); usually, it's the former addressing the latter. The speaker can be portrayed/interpreted as the lover (*a'shiq*), and the addressee as the beloved (*ma'shooq*). Unlike the Sapphic lyric which invokes a god or a goddess to intervene on behalf of the supplicant, the narrator of a kafi deliberately blurs the distinction between divine (*haqiqi*) and temporal (*mijazi*) love to express the anguish of separation (*faraq*) and yearning for union or oneness (*wahdat*). The murshid–murid relationship seamlessly translates into God–human, lover–beloved and even Heer–Ranjha, the ill-fated lovers of the most famous Punjabi folk tale. The erotic serves as the predicate for the numinous and vice versa.

Dr Mohan Singh Diwana, an early-twentieth-century Punjabi scholar, is acknowledged as the undisputed saviour of Hussein's kafis in written form. He discovered 138 kafis in a collection of Hindu, Muslim and Sikh mystical poetry by an unknown Sindhi editor. The collection was in Gurmukhi script and published in Lahore around 1900. These kafis, along with the twenty-five he found in a handwritten Gurmukhi manuscript in the Punjab University library (manuscript #374, dated 1804, the oldest textual record of Hussein's work), made up the first Urdu script edition of Hussein's poetry published in 1942. As more editions followed, new kafis were discovered and contributed, the number of kafis rose, and the differences between the various versions of kafis, ranging from minor to major, started to emerge.

Modern Pakistani scholars, especially working in the Urdu tradition, lament the adulteration of kafis by ignoramus singers and qawwals who are deemed responsible for circulating varying versions that undermine the authenticity of Hussein's work. These critics and scholars overlook the contribution of these devotional singers, the sole guarantors of an oral tradition who helped Hussein's poetry survive the Mughal, British and postcolonial vicissitudes. We, the modern readers, owe a great deal to the illiterate minstrel caste, derogatorily known as the *mirasis*, who celebrated these kafis as expressions of love, loss and, let's admit it, devotion and reverence. They preserved not only the song, but also the verve and warmth that escape the objective, and often sterile, scholarly translations.

Perhaps, Hussein, the saint, is in a better position to defend his own literary legacy as well as counter two other contemporary developments.

Firstly, the appropriation of spirituality by the slick Mammon of late capitalism is reflected in the popularity of Sufi music produced and marketed by Coke Studio, a Coca-Cola-sponsored entertainment venture. The Studio has provided a forum for Pakistani artists to fuse classical, folk and modern rhythms into catchy tunes, all the rage on the radio, fashion-show runways and in the music collections of the urban youth. I must admit, I'm among the first to download as soon as the new season of Coke Studio is available online, yet the subversion of mystical poetry into subtle advertisement for a corporate brand should not be lost on the listener.

Secondly, Hussein, the saint, is a bulwark against the puritanical Wahabi ideology fuelled by the petrodollars of Gulf sheikhdoms running amok in present-day Pakistan. No wonder the Sufi shrines, viewed as the hashish-clouded dens of singing and dancing, are high on the list of the God-opiated aspirants of martyrdom with a penchant for suicide blasts.

Apologia

Why translate a text of poetry? To express an affinity towards a kindred sensibility, to discover and explore a poetic process and (re)examine one's own aesthetics, to recall, revive a song through the sounds of a different language while preserving its emotional vitality.

A single wrong weave may not go well with the Master

(kafi 136)

I felt the jitters of a novice translator when I got to this line towards the end of this project. A moment to take stock, a moment to reckon. Did the poet in me go too far, overplaying the music over the message? What I found in Hussein's work was not the moral piety of a saint confined to a particular religious tradition, but the defiant devotion of a sixteenth-century poet upholding the nonconformist values of spirituality. And what I have attempted to (re)produce is not a literal translation, but the poetry of Shah Hussein. If I misread a line, misunderstood the theme, misinterpreted a word, if my efforts were tainted by ego and ambition, forgive me, Murshid.

In the end we all settle in dust (kafis 22, 32, 59, 70, 77); *the wretched grave, your native land* (kafi 124); *a few feet of burial ground, all the property you need* (kafis 48, 74). This is a recurring reminder in Hussein's kafis. Visit the mausoleums of the Mughal sovereigns, the marvels of architecture, the marble floors, the floral mosaics, the ornate domes, the once gem-studded graves. The tomb of Jehangir in Shahdara, Madho's hometown, is a vast complex of sprawling lawns imitating the geometry of a Persian paradise. Unfortunately, due to lack of proper conservation, the place is in a sorry state of disrepair; patchy repair work here and there, dry fountains, littered grounds and barely a trace of tall spruces along the cobbled paths treaded by the tourists around this forlorn grandeur. Compare this to the modest shrine of Shah Hussein in Baghbanpura near another dilapidated wonder of the Mughal era, the Shalimar Gardens. The side-by-side graves of Hussein and Madho are always heaped with fresh rose and marigold garlands offered by the daily throngs of devotees. The last week of March 2016 will mark the 428th *urs* of Shah Hussein, aka Madho Lal Hussein. The celebration is commonly known as *Mela Chiraga'an*, the Festival of Lamps. It makes one wonder: Who *does* finally settle in dust, and who remains fragrant and illuminated?

Lahore
August 2015

KAFIS

1

O God, you are the only confidant of my days
You are inside, outside, you are settled in my pores
You the warp, the weft, my each and everything is you
Says Hussein, the worthless fakir, I am nothing, You are all

2

My colourful spinning wheel I painted red
Bigger grew the wheel, greater the weave
            Twelve years passed
For the sake of my Sain these eyes weep
            and weeping worsens my state
Bigger the wheel, wider the spins
They all came to get their hair done
No one came to share my sorrows
No one willing to go along
A calf ate up the cotton ball
All my neighbours raised a ruckus
What did I do wrong? They all went after me
Bigger the wheel, heavier the basket my parents placed
on my head. Says Hussein, the fakir of the Sain,
            take good care of what you carry

                        ~

Variation

Pretty red I painted my loom, my plaything

Happily I reached my pubescence
Now I weep, and weeping
worsens my sorry state
Pretty spins my wheel, attracts
weavers far and wide. No one asks
why you weep. No one offers
        to take me yonder
The handsome weavers
whet my lust, provoke
the complaints of neighbours
What did I do to madden
the whole damn neighbourhood?
O my mother, O my father
why did you teach me to spin
yarns that dazzle and condemn?
Says Hussein, the Sain's fakir,
        you better take care of
your wheel night and day

3

Come, let's dance the *luddi*
Grab that string and let high your kite
My string in my lover's hand, I'm his kite
You'll regret the moment you find yourself in a pit
Says Hussein, the Sain's fakir, the whole world drowns

4

Sorrows are our completion, I tell you,
aches and scars compose a being
Those busy turning millions to billions
        remain greedy as ever
Your white robe is fuel for fire
You may have been better off
with a dervish's grimy cloak
Those who keep the company
        of the plain and simple
stay out of harm's way and arrive
        at fuller wisdom
Says Hussein, the Sain's fakir,
People leave unfulfilled

5

My Master, I'm yours, and I'm done for
Don't you ever erase me from your heart
I've given up all the rest. I have no virtue,
        no skill. Bless me and I'll be free
Keep me as you like, my lovely one,
I've sought refuge in your shade
If only you'd give a favourable glance
I'm up here asleep on the top floor,
windows wide open in all directions
Says Hussein, the Sain's devotee,
I'm the bitch at your doorstep

6

All night I sobbed. The tears
neither diluted nor dissolved
the ache. Can't trust
this breath, life is a night
spent in a tavern. Soul
sheds the body, the festival
disperses like autumn leaves
Says Hussein, the Sain's fakir,
before you know it, dawn breaks

7

Time to invoke, girl, let's rise and praise Ram
Regretfully you'll rub your palms over lost time
Many had their fill at this riverbank
You too took your fair share
This one's not done yet, that one's filled up
This one home, that one still on her way
Says Hussein, the Sain's fakir, come
where the women gather for work

8

Why should they worry, folks,
those who got the Sain by their side
They fared well those who loved God for long
Carrying the amorous load they announced door to door
Says Hussein, the Sain's fakir, I found my boxful of love!
Why should they be worried, folks, those who got the Sain?
Bless them, why should they worry about anything?

9

One day you'll remember the hometown alleys
Bees fly off the flowers, branches shed their leaves
Only the inflamed knows the flame. The rest is idle chatter
Get away, scholar, the heart is not satisfied
Talkers talk the impossible

10

Go wherever dwells my Sweetheart
Go there and say let me be humbled
For your sake I'll sacrifice myself
Once I find you I'll be refreshed
Painful nights, sorrowful days
Death's become an obligation
My undone braids wrapped around the neck
I've turned into a wandering woman
searching the cities and the wilderness
Out of shame I don't cry out loud
Says Hussein, the Sain's fakir,
I lie awake night and day

~

Variation

Go wherever dwells the Sweetheart
Go there and ask: Is it time?

Go tell him: Nights are a pain,
the days full of anxiety.
Death's become obligatory.

I turn gypsy, put on
the heavy brass anklets.
My braids undone, my hair
wrapped around the neck
I walk into the flickering mirages.
He'll dust off my ashes,
embrace and refresh me.

I shan't let out a cry lest you be defamed.
Says Hussein, the worthless devotee,
I lie awake night and day.

11

If you were a lover, you'd earn love
The path of love is a needle's eye
Be a thread, go through
Outwardly pious, sordid within:
What a great man of learning you make!
Says Hussein, if you free yourself from all honours,
only then you can achieve that special honour

12

Beware of the end, O Fellow!
You squandered your life, now left with nothing
At your doorstep arrive the travelling merchants
You purchase a few trinkets on a loan
As much as you can, try to find the hidden
Says Hussein, the Sain's fakir, don't
get entangled in honour and dishonour

13

My lover grabbed my arm
Why would I ask him to let go?
Dark night drizzling, painful
the approaching hour of departure
You'll know what love's all about
once it seeps into your bones
Why dig a well in brackish soil?
Why sow a seed in sand?
You, who are making giant leaps,
one day you'll be leapt over, my man!
Says Hussein, the humble fakir,
look into the lover's eyes, and let
the gaze remain interlocked

14

The customer's leaving, earn something
Don't let him go empty-handed even if
you lose a penny or two in the bargain
Only a few days left at the father's house
turn your attention towards the Sain
Learn to weave a few yarns otherwise
You'll remain a dowry-less spinster
You ask strangers for loans
Get something out of the friend
Says Hussein, the lowly fakir,
take this advice from the wise

15

Try to understand, you fool,
where's home, try to understand
You are a rascal, your intellect self-serving,
who'd call you wise? On these paths I've seen
the nobles, royals, sultans passing
He kills and He raises the dead
Izrael is merely an excuse
Says Hussein, the Sain's fakir,
without any reason we depart

16

Lay me, slay me, play me
I sacrifice my all for you, Sain
They mock me if I fall silent
I'm ruined if I dare speak
You make one beg for morsels
For the other you host feasts
One giggles in the lover's arms
the other is miserable without the husband
I'm not deserving, yet quick to claim you
Says Hussein, the Sain's fakir, I'll get
safely across the waters
if you're watching over

17

This talk of lovers, Girlfriend, is torture
till my man finds his way home
Separation set me on fire
and I grew to know myself better
Childhood I wasted in games and play
Youth lost to pride and vanity
What a waste: my beauty. If only
I'd learned how to please my lover
Constantly I smoulder upon the embers
The sorrow won't leave the heart
Craving for his sight burns me up
She's the chosen one, says Hussein,
      for whom comes the groom

18

My little heart
got so attached to you
Can't break off even if I tried
Can't let go even if I left
Ordained to be yours forever
The Sain opened up his treasuries
I too spread out my tattered sack
How long can I keep the lamp of reason
lit through the stormy separation?
Some stand first, some arrive second,
Shah Hussein stumbling at the very end

19

O Girlfriend, I trusted my eyes
Those with the pure looks
can never be deceived
Black silk can never be dyed white
Who ever heard of a white crow?
They are the true martyrs:
those who die for the beloved

20

My love, I walked past the streams,
thirsty. Good that the sweet molasses
            got consumed by the flies
I was saved from the ceaseless drone
Good the dogs licked off the water container
I bathed in the pond's fresh and clear waters
Says Hussein, the Sain's fakir, there came
an abyss, I jumped over, there came
a hoop, I jumped through

21

Dear Lal! How can this life be trusted?
The bee becomes a stranger to the flower,
        flies off into the unknown
This world a lie, this existence an illusion,
like a dewdrop mistaken for a pearl
        Those who took care of my lover
need not fear death. Says Hussein, the Sain's fakir,
don't you worry about the body, a disposable vessel

22

The world we leave behind
To the world we won't return
The deeds, good or evil, determine
whatever our next placement
First the birth then the death
Sweet friends sew our shroud
drive us down to the grave-end
For a few days we live and prosper
Who knows when we'll be turned over?
On whose shoulders we'd be carried?
Like kids we amuse ourselves for now
Limbs tied to a pole later we'll be carried
Says Hussein, the devotee of the Sain,
Arrogance, the greatest mendacity
Back into the dust we settle

23

May I be sacrificed upon you, please
spare some pity for the humble ones
Nights are torture, days an exhaustion
Despair rages like a caged lion
Scarf tied around my neck, humbly
I touch your feet: be mine, I beg
For you I've laid down my head
Into you I have dissolved my being
Says Hussein, the Sain's fakir,
I trust no one except you
Come, hold me, my love

24

To offer my heart I go. I'll sacrifice
my all to anyone who belongs
to the same town as my beloved
Once he settled in my heart
no room was left for another
The whole wide world I searched
No one could please me like you
Shah Hussein lies at your doorstep, Sain,
      yearning for your name

25

Let's live, next to the lover let's live,
Litany of sins, heaps of mockery: let's bear it all,
living close to the lover. If they sever off the head
let's not betray a single whisper, only share
with those whose words are our medicine
If there's sandalwood in my own courtyard
why should I go out seeking any fragrance
Says Hussein, the Sain's fakir, better
finish yourself off while you're still alive

26

Life passed day by day
not for a moment I remembered
So busy weaving, not a yard I saved
Blank papers I kept filling
not a word I wrote worth the ink
The rippling ponds I passed
never drank a single cupped palm
Says Hussein, the beggar-wanderer
never said farewell before departure

27

O girl going by, your beauty is a lie
You won't flaunt your colourful bangles for long
You won't repeat your youth. Laugh then,
play, amuse your Sweetheart before
the grave-dirt fills your mouth
Says Hussein, the lowly fakir,
eventually the will of the Almighty. Pack up
your bags, girl, if you want to come along

28

Let's celebrate, enjoy for a while
What use the pride in wealth and youth that makes
        wise men fall afoul their wisdom?
My girlfriends, my childhood playmates, all left,
        all settled in strangers' houses
The carefree days at your parents'
        you will miss in your dreams
Says Hussein, the Sain's fakir, let's do
        the good that can be done

29

Careful, Girlfriend, be very careful
handling the red wedding dress
Married women came to see my precious dress
They left full of praises. The neighbour woman
came and asked for the dress I left hanging
I couldn't let go for a moment. The dress
someone carried across the snows
all the way from Kashmir. The dress
someone brought from Gujarat
to dispel the virgin's fear of the first night
The dress bought in Multan, only God knows
where it came from, just embrace
the sleeping one, my love
My fine dress dyed red with rare pigments
No confidant can I find. Where's my husband?
To the dress I added the head scarf, the rest
up to the Sain, I can't do anything else
Every bride owns a wedding dress
They're all the branches of the same tree
but you're the incomparable bride
The dress fades as I roam place to place

My wedding gown being woven
while Krishna played by the Jamuna
The path ahead steep and rugged
Says Hussein, the wanderer,
the night descends upon the wilderness
and the Almighty remains indifferent

30

You better spin this, foolish girl,
Focus only on spinning
You wasted your whole life
Not a single woven spool in your basket
You sashay up and down the alleys heedlessly
Says Hussein, the Sain's fakir, there goes
                the one without a trousseau

31

Let me be sacrificed upon you
again and again, you may take my all
The lover who's become the source
of my mockery, he's my Master, I his slave
Suddenly I was caught unawares
My parents' house seemed an abode of strangers
Says Hussein, the worthless fakir,
I won't recognize another except you
I'm the dirt of your feet, I'm the trampled

32

We won't return to this world again
Not forever the mustard blooms
Not forever rains the monsoon
Thoughtful must be our actions
to save us from reaping regrets
Says Hussein, loud and clear,
eventually we'll all settle in dust

33

O Mama let me play a while
When shall I get another chance?
I'm not worth much to begin with
On top of it I forget the lesson
My lover, so skilful and handsome,
will he embrace or not touch at all?
God, my heart anxiously trembles
Life's short and the world full of guiles
Thus went the prime of my youth
My life spent in ignorance, fate runs its course
Shah Hussein, the Sain's fakir, whatever happens
        will happen by the will of God
Finally you've got to go from here to there
That's when you'll be regretful

34

I got no play, so passed the night
All are high and mighty, mine the lowest lineage
To be the player or the plaything, so arrived the dawn
The boat caught in a whirlpool, called out the boatman
Shah Hussein's humility cuts like an axe

35

Why should you worry if you got the lover by your side?
The beautiful face of the Sweetheart dissolved in my eyes
Not for a moment does he leave me, the one
          who lives within
Says Hussein, the Sain's fakir, we got to go today or tomorrow

36

Why don't you get it, foolish girl, your time's passing by
This life lasts a day or two, passes in the blink of an eye
Wealth, property, treasures, no one takes along
Mother, father, brother, spouse, no one comes along
Says Hussein, the worthless fakir, only
       the Sain's name remains

37

Why such self-importance, Hussein?
Who do you think you are? You are
a weed among the garden's fancy flowers
Never did you know thyself and yet
you compare yourself to others
Deep the ocean of love that made
        Mansoor embrace his cross
Shah Hussein lies at the doorstep
hoping to be lifted and embraced

38

God, pay no attention to my flaws
This sinful one got no skills, all filled up with follies
Keep me any way you wish, Sweetheart
I'm stretched out at your doorway
Be kind, begs Hussein,
judging this lowly fakir

39

Spin the wheel, girl, so says Mother
Spin it, says my naïve mother
I've always been spinning
I've been pierced by a spear
I lost all my senses
Smashed up the loom, lost the thread
I've kicked away the basket
They all cry the usual tears
only the lovers cry blood
Says Hussein loud and clear:
You won't return here again

40

One, two, three, four, five,
six, seven . . . we were eight, nine
All went home carrying their handlooms
        I'm left all alone
The kind of fabric you weave
is the kind of sheet stretched over your sleep
Says Hussein, the Sain's fakir,
        we whet the lust of death

41

What makes you think you'll be
        the delight of your darling?
Never swept the garbage piled inside
Better learn how to spin, foolish girl
All you seek are the wedding celebrations
The thread's come apart, the spindle
lies broken, better worry about the jenny
Says Hussein, the Sain's fakir, nothing
        but suffering for the unprepared

42

Go round and round, O Handloom
May she live, the one who spins you
May she live, the one who spools you
        Shah Hussein, you dotard,
gaps widen between your teeth, rise
and search for them in the morning
the ones who left since the twilight
Breathe in and out the Master's name
Only then will you find your balance
In the rhythm of the circling loom
hear the call and the answer
Says Hussein, the Sain's fakir,
        I'm nothing, You are all

43

Be fearful as long as you live
In the bazaar of love, poor monkeys
put to bizarre tricks. Not easy, I tell you,
to entertain the whims of the beloved
Don't be a stubborn colt, bow down
Lovers risk life and reputation
Grab the flame through the fire
Sighs 'n' sobs, that's not the way
Out in the field you discover love
Not easy to catch a glimpse. Pluck out
the heart at the glint of love's blade
The real lover first finishes off the body
Not easy starting up passion, but once started
better not tell anyone. Without the beloved
it's a false game of a gossip spun world
Don't seek the temporal out of truth
Don't ignore one or the other
Says Hussein, the beggar fakir,
what can you do if he remains indifferent?
Let him sort what he started. Look!
Here comes the wedding party

44

O dissembler of embarrassments,
Don't pay attention to my flaws
You the omnipotent sultan, you know
the true state of my heart. Nothing remains
hidden from you, don't expose this poor woman
You are intelligent, you are wise, you my only protector
You know every detail of what I think, what I feel
You the giver, the forgiver, the ever generous
You the river of kindness when beggars yearn to be near
Let his heart float in your stream, begs Hussein
He'll be saved from pain and sorrow if he offers
gratitude for each and every moment

45

Anywhere you look
there's deceit and deception
Nowhere a trickle of peace
Hussein, go solitary in fraudulent times
Heart desires a lover, body seeks calm
Between the two tyrants how can you
     row your boat, Hussein?

46

Why did I join this weaving session?
Not a single thread can I string
Started playing as soon as I arrived,
ignored the loom. The ox sniffs
the balls of wool I brought to spin
The other girls disentangle and spool
This miserable one is caught in cotton
The rest wove their yards of cloth
What do I have to show for myself?
Says Hussein, only the skilful girls
          get to embrace the lover

47

Don't ever forget God, O Woman,
that's the prayer of mendicants
You may forget all, but God is not worth forgetting
Gold and beauty—short living. Love never decays
You laugh and play with the rest then why act so formal
with the lover? Two pairs of eyes met and acquiesced
then what's the need of a go-between? Love settled
in your courtyard, how could you have any worry?
I swear by my mother, I swear by my father:
Love, the best devotion. The youth you're so proud of
will be reduced to ashes. Says Hussein, the Master's fakir,
if you accept your mortality then why the pride?

48

Why do you strut the land, fellow?
You dress well, you eat gourmet,
you fatten the lamb for death
A few feet of burial ground
is all the property you need
Why occupy and accumulate
the acres you can't own?
Says Hussein, the Master's fakir,
in the end we mix with dirt

49

My shirt soaked with tears
The mistakes I make spinning
I blame on the faulty loom
'I'm coming, I'm coming,' he said
Twelve months have passed since
This dark little cottage
and no friend around
Blackbuck, you grazed
the borders of Shah Hussein's fields
The Writer of Fate ordained
Now what's the use of crying

50

Among my skilled girlfriends
I am the one without any talent
The mountains cower
before the fearsome Sahib
Who am I, the pitiful one?
The lover sent me and I forgot
the errand I was sent for
The girls get together, fix
trousseaus for their weddings
The lovely me remained a spinster
O girlfriends, says Hussein, misery
if you haven't done your work

51

After the spell of youth I reflected . . .
O God, may I never lose your mercy
Monsoon arrives, girlfriends set up
the swings, celebrate the rain festival
The river's deep, the raft decrepit
Only God can get me across
This one spinning, that one spooling
this one pining for a husband
that one glows in her lover's arms
Says Hussein, the miserable mendicant,
they all make false promises

52

Come home, the grave calls you
Anyone who arrives, can't stay
whether king, lord, or nobleman
Let the Master settle in each breath
That's the trick, that's the hope
Says Hussein, the humble fakir,
in the end we all settle in dust

53

Can't stay here, let's prepare for departure
You raise mansions, tall and mighty,
the wretched grave your real home
You take such pride in the body,
it will wane like the shade of a tree
Stop being clever, try being gentle,
fear the Almighty. Says Hussein, the fakir,
if you seek life then die before dying

54

In this world life's short
who's got time for entanglements?
Horses, elephants, temples, wealth
how long can anyone claim anything?
Where the mullah, the magistrate,
where the mighty armies of the past?
This world lasts a day or two, my dear,
always beware of the name that matters
Says Hussein, the Sain's fakir, it's all
        a merchandise of lies

55

Play your childhood games, girl,
today or tomorrow you return to the in-laws
Play your rag ball, girl, dangle your gold earring
To the in-laws you must go, your parents' home an illusion
The monsoon enlivens, the vines sprawl wide
Says Hussein, the Sain's fakir, today
you've come, tomorrow you're gone

56

O God, I hid my weaver's tools
You are merciful, Sain
With rings on my finger
how can I do any labour?
With my red velvet shoes
how can I sit still and weave?
For the sake of warming the stove
I sweat for the five measly *kaseera*s
How can I pay for the expenses?
Inside I'm a den of hens, outside
the serenity of a peacock
Says Hussein, the Sain's fakir,
the good weaving girl got
kidnapped by the robbers

57

Nothing pleases me except my lover
My body a clay oven, my sighs
the flames. Heat rises, burns
my body and heart. The body knows
what it wants. The heart is aware
of its desires. If only I had
a confidant to guess my passion
Says Hussein, the Sain's fakir,
the envious folk quarrel brazenly

58

Judgement based on deeds
whether a pious Sufi or a lowly *bhangi*
Whatever God wants that's what
happens, this the worthy truth
He calls himself one, he calls himself
many. He's a multicoloured Master
Says Hussein, she's the real bride
who dyes herself in the lover's colours

59

It's a selfishly motivated world
That's the truth, O Fakir
Motives come, motives go
Motives draw the crowds
to the doorsteps of holy men
Motives make the generous
feed the hungry, clothe the naked
No one offers a glass of water
without an ulterior motive
Says Hussein, he's the shah
of shahs, the selfless one
who acts free of all motives

60

Where did you come from, girl?
Why create such a ruckus? You wasted
your own yarn, now you blame the weaver
Distracted you sat at the loom, now you carry
your five sickly spindles. You stand
in the market haggling with the merchants
Why shed tears after losing the bargain?
You frolicked around with the girlfriends,
forgot all about the lover. Why take up
a load that makes difficult the road?
Says Hussein, the wretched fakir:
Did you ever think of dying?

61

Round and round goes the world
and you go along, O Wanderer
As long as you follow the five senses
what fame will you find, O Vagabond?
The choicest fruits you pick
turn out to be bitter berries
Steep the slope, tortuous the trail,
long the journey of seekers
You wasted life conning and collecting
No millionaire or billionaire ever escaped
death's angel. Bless the comers, bless the goers
Says Hussein, the Sain's fakir, I kiss
        the feet of my Master

62

Among the moons of a thousand worlds
who do you think you are, girl?
You been grazing the lambs
You been shearing the wool
And when you ascend a steep slope
thorns pierce your dainty feet. Never seen
anyone like you. After coming this far
now you're turning back
Without proper preparation
men stumble down the dark
Even prophets, saints, holy men
lie entombed and enshrined
They all had their fill, they all
filled up their colourful pitchers
Shah Hussein, the poor fakir,
stands waiting at the door

63

Does it matter if I'm good or bad?
All that matters: I'm your woman, Master
Foolish folk call me crazy. I'm dyed
            in my Master's colours
My lover has settled in my eyes
I roam the alleys, intoxicated
Says Hussein, the Sain's fakir, I am
betrothed to the most beautiful beau

64

O God, a basket between my knees
merrily I weave, keep on weaving
My body a lyre, my veins the strings,
      I chant Sain, Sain
My heart's content my passion's true
Says Hussein, the Sain's fakir,
I tied myself to you. Take me
      all the way

65

I'll be the servant of truth seekers,
do the scullion jobs: cook, clean,
             wash the dirty dishes
I collect the leaves of pipal trees
and people think I'm crazy
What would people know
I'm speared by separation
Far and wide folks have heard of Heer
the woman who refused the world
for the sake of love. They're touched,
they're moved, but what do they do for me?
I'm the slave girl bought by my swarthy lover
        My dark lover, my Sain
Says Hussein, the wretched fakir,
spare a glance for the smouldering one

66

He may dye my life
into any colour he likes
Fortunate are the ones
fated to be fakir wanderers
The needle of wisdom, the thread
of love stitches together true friends
Says Hussein, the Sain's fakir,
thrones aren't granted upon asking

67

The night about to pass
I haven't lured home my lover
Praise the bride resting
in the arms of her man
The last of the lamps flickers
in my dark little cottage
Death leads me by the arm
No friend, no companion
Slept away the night, you tramp,
The fortunate one stayed up
Those consumed by the ardour
become aware, remain awake
Girlfriends, says Hussein,
the only way to get your man:
nightlong servitude of the Master

68

Swaying and sashaying, O Mother
Praise Ram, I pranced all the way to the groom
The in-laws mock me for being a brazen bride
O naïve Mama, no needlework I learned,
how would I embroider a thing?
I learned no skills at my parents' house
Diddled around with a bare spindle
The fellow weaver girls, my confidantes,
left me all to myself. Nothing I could do
when the guards of the Almighty came
They left me, my real brothers. Alone
I occupy the wedding stage
Says Hussein, the wretched fakir,
I've come here clueless

69

We won't return, naïve Mother
This is the time, the only chance
Do yourself a favour: recite
His name again and again
When I was single my only wish:
to be handed over to a stranger
Little did I know of the stratagems
mastered by the fortunate few
         to outwit sorrows
Chaupat has eighty-four squares
Only the winner remains unharmed
Little did I know of clever ruses
Hussein tells it like the truth:
Comforts and joys as long as you live
The afterlife riddled with regrets

70

O arrogant one
count the breath as a blessing
What did you bring? What will you take?
Impermanent the world and its contents
Short the stay, unpredictable life,
        don't be so proud
Says Hussein, the lowly fakir,
in the end we all settle in dust

71

Life is too short
for grievance against anyone
No matter what direction I turn
Death is in the way. No one
speaks of life. Everyone must go,
            no exception, no extension
Says Hussein, the Sain's fakir,
            death weaves the lasso

72

I must go to Ranjha's village
Someone please come along
I beg, I plead, but I'll have to go
all alone. The river's deep,
the raft falling apart, wild animals
occupy the landing. I'll give
my fingers' precious rings if anyone
brings news of my friend
Nights are a pain, agonizing days
Fresh the wound inflicted by the Friend
Ranjha, my lover, known as a healer
My body suffers strange aches
Says Hussein, the humble fakir,
Sain sends the messages

~

Variation (after listening to Pathanay Khan sing this kafi)

They call me a stubborn child,
pestering. I shall mewl for weeks

till someone leads me to Ranjhra.

No one takes me seriously. I unfurl
my despair, throw myself at their feet.
I beg, I plead—Better accept

I'll have to make it all alone.
Wretched me, what can I do?
Sain sends the messages . . .

Deep the waters, a beaten raft,
the wild ones prowl the banks.
Sain sends the messages . . .

Take my rings, take my bracelets,
Take anything I hold precious, bring
some news of my Ranjhra . . .

Save your medicines, fellows,
send for Ranjhra, my ache,
my cure, my river, my raft.

73

O Mother, don't even start
about a suitable suitor
I'm Ranjha's, Ranjha's mine
The Kheras can wait in vain
People think Heer has gone crazy
Heer's lover is a servant
Says Hussein, the Sain's devotee,
only the flawless God knows better

74

Know thyself, Fellow
Easier to find Sain
if you know who *you* are
Golden castles, silver jewels
end up at the cremation ground
Whether you're aware or not
the angel of death intrigues
above your head. A few feet
for the grave is all you need
Why seek a greater entitlement?
Gold, silver, wealth, treasure
come and stay around like guests
Says Hussein, the wretched fakir,
give up the self-delusions

75

The whole world knows
how I long to meet you, Sain
All I want is to stay by your side forever
Do let me see you. The syllables of your name,
        the morsels I feed my breath
Says Hussein, the wretched fakir,
        You the Master, I the slave

76

Mother, change if you can
the course of my fate
In a bridal palanquin
Kheras carry me away
I'm weak, I'm helpless
Ranjha hooked me
set storms in my heart
The Almighty holds the string
I squirm like a fish
Says Hussein, the Sain's fakir,
False is the strength of Kheras

77

O Life, what are you so proud of?
In the end you'll mix with dirt
The world you must leave for sure
The perfumed princes, nobles, kings:
fuel for the sandalwood-scented pyres
The merrymakers may have their fun,
barefoot they'll be carried upon the biers
No privileges or favours, indifference
reigns in the Master's house. You'll answer
the questions you ask of yourself,
says Hussein, the wretched fakir

78

Few are the days, girl,
your friends are here to play
Naive mother won't let me play
Painful tears drip from my eyes
In the moonlight my friends play
In the dark I spend my hours
From the parents to the in-laws
they must go, all brides are aware
Says Hussein, the wretched fakir,
the ones who commit
stay faithful forever

The house full of pretty girlfriends
They don't listen, they don't heed
In the mud they prefer to slither
Some hungry, some thirsty
some asleep, some awake,
some loud, some silent
All five aloft the flood waters
All five the same. Someone
brought them all together
in a house they know so well
The bride who knows how to
tame these five is the one
who makes happy her husband
Says Hussein, the host of senses,
suddenly blows the wind

80

The nights you sleep off
The days you spend loafing
You love fun and play, my little Life
Sometimes rise and recite Ram in the morning
Short is your stay at the parents. Soon
you must return to the in-laws. Any day now
the *muklaroos* will be here to fetch the newly-wed
No one to blame, says Hussein, the Sain's fakir,
you only get one chance, my little Life

81

Hear this one plea of the miserable, O Life!
The warp of wisdom, the weft of devotion
weave into every pelt, O Life
Why worry? What use the idle talk?
You lose if you don't sing of Ram
You reap whatever you sow
What use the pride in youth?
The lords of lords and sultans
all got picked by the goddess of death
Says Hussein, the wandering fakir,
You gave up the thread and loom, O Life
Now you shall meet the groom

82

Ever reckoned, dear fellow, one day you'll die?
You sleep day and night upon a bed of illusion
False the quilt, false the pillow
Only for a few days this nomad soul
sojourns in a house of bones
Says Hussein, the God's fakir,
humility is the path to the Sain

83

Hey you, listen: the death calls
Recite God's name, the customer leaves
Fearless the fish dwells in the deep sea
For one such fish reaches the net
The kings, princes, nobles, aristocrats
waving their lances, blowing their horns
in a blink the death annihilates
The multistoreyed houses, the ornamentations
Death makes the dwellers homeless in a moment
Life's a sparrow, death the hunter lying in wait
Today and tomorrow he pounces on you
Says Hussein, the wretched fakir:
        False is man's pride

84

Now I shall weave you the way I like, O little life of mine,
my pampered princeling, my mortal darling,
      I shall weave you
in patterns of my choice. All this time I spent
      spinning and spooling
the useless thread. A weaver woman tied to the loom
I worked my spindles despite the detractors
What would they know of plain, twill, satin?
Only the tool tells a thousand entanglements
I know the warp, know the weft, know the old loom
Nothing I need to say, I know what I know
Only a few inches wide the distance between
the earth and sky where dwell the divinities
Everyone reached the crystal palace
except Hussein, the wretched

85

It makes sense, the talk of keeping a commitment
Like a candle's moth do not flinch while burning
Love cudgels and tames the wild beast of passion
Says Hussein, the Sain's devotee, preserve the love ties

86

My sweet lover's face, fresh in my heart day and night
Yours the garden, yours the grove, I'm your nightingale
If I can be my lover's delight then no plaything do I need
Says Hussein, the wretched fakir, I'm the dirt of his doorstep

87

What will he do with this wretched woman?
I neither sheared nor wove, what share can I claim
of the woven cloth? The premonition of the oil press
makes the sesame seeds cry oily tears at birth
Your bones pressed six feet under
will end your boastful swagger
Says Hussein, the God's fakir,
versify the veracity

88

I'm the lowly cleaner at the esteemed house
Attentively I sieve, meditatively I sweep
I dust away the lust, envy, anger
The judge knows, the ruler knows
free from the jobs I work voluntarily
The sheriff knows, the registrar knows
I serve no one except my Master
Says Hussein, the wretched fakir,
I yearn to see your face

89

Come, girl, let's dance the *jhumar*
Come, girl, let's praise Ram
Do let us enjoy, Mother, the few days
we got at home. We won't get another chance
We yearn for the beloved, let jealous folk gossip
To meet the lover, our first and foremost desire
The girlfriends settled in high mansions
What did they do to get there?
An empty spindle left in my hand
Muklaroo seated at the doorstep
My girlfriends sway upon the swings
hanging down the tall pipal trees
And I'm here on my own
Says Hussein, the wretched fakir,
you'll leave the world, you'll die
When will you ever look within?

90

Let me stand and watch for a few days
the polo tournament. Who wins, who loses,
whose brisk horse makes a clever move?
Let's see who dares a score. The games
this heart must endure. Let's see who hits the ball
across the field. The crowd cheers and jeers
My dear Shah Hussein, do you realize
          what's at stake here?

91

The nights stretched longer without the lover
Ranjha's gypsy, I'm the gypsy woman
        known for her crazy devotion
The skin wrinkles, the skeleton rattles
Naïve me, what would I know of passion
The separation pulls tight its strings
Says Hussein, the devotee of the Sain,
I'm woven into your shirt's pattern

92

You are a momentary guest, traveller
All possessions you must leave behind
The famous lords of the castles vanish
Only their profiles are left engraved on coins
Get rid of pride, seek humility. No one belongs
anywhere. Says Hussein, the wretched fakir,
        breathe to the rhythm of Sain, Sain

93

Why would they sit around spinning,
those who are in love, O Friend?
Why would a girl in swoon sit at the loom?
You fall in love, you discard proprieties,
you forget the five times prayers
Wounded and dazed roams the mad girl
leaving her loom untended. Long time
        I've loved my Sweetheart
Loved him before I grew my tresses
Says Hussein, the lowly fakir,
the Sain dyes my eyes red

Rendezvous with the lover—now you're talking!
Far is Ranjha, quick! We must swim across
The fierce ocean roils, let's seek
the help of holy ones. I'll turn
gypsy for the sake of Sain. I'll do
whatever can be done. If the lover comes
I'll distribute sweets worth millions
The lover embraces, all gets illuminated,
the moment of gratitude. Says Hussein,
if you seek life, die while still alive

95

Repeat 'Sain, Sain' even if the parents forbid
Start a romance, make the lover homebound
Heer was in love since infancy. Desperately
she turned in her cradle, no respite for a moment
Like a butcher with his slaughter knife
the agony of separation rips into the veins
The troubles of a hundred years gone
        once Ranjha glances her way

95 (A)

Yearning for Ranjha pierced the body
Thorns turned into my confidants
The cutters, clippers, pliers, tongs all broke
Hundreds of mullahs, hundreds of wise men,
hundreds of scholars tried in vain. Not till
       Ranjha appears
Heer delivered from her woes

96

Deep waters ahead, how shall I get across?
Dark night, long journey, no companion
I quarrel with the boatman
He's right, I'm wrong. Who can I ask for help?
My girlfriends dally with lovers, leaving me alone
Says Hussein, the wretched fakir, I cry
wasting the hours at hand

May I be sacrificed upon you, my Sain, my sweet confidant
Do visit me sometime, my constant helper, my flaw concealer
This one wish I ask of you, ever increase my longing for you
Says Hussein, the lowly fakir, you are my constant fulfilment

98

Fun and games, my fate: so ordained the God
Some cried, some merrily left the playground
Set aside pride, get hold of humility
What did the self ever serve you?
Says Hussein, the devotee of the Sain,
leave this world safe and sound

99

Difficult the shores of dispossession
        Place it in a crucible, melt
the damned intellect, purify the flesh
Get rid of pride, adopt kindness, take up
        the path of sweetness
Says Hussein, the lowly fakir, tear up
        the ledger of saintly business

100

Blame the bearers, Mother,
for rushing ahead my palanquin
The travellers pass you by carrying
load upon load, and you never
packed up your bags. This one
about to depart, that one sitting ready
Death stands at your head and you drool
over the gardens blooming in spring
Says Hussein, the lowly fakir,
someone please turn around
and explain to these friends

101

Not easy to hear the truth, Mister
Why tolerate the truth when lies
seep and settle down in the bones?
Those who heard the truth
caught a spark and flared
The lover has burnt the veil,
embarrassed the envious rivals
Poisonous cobras slither in the alleys
Unharmed the one who embraced her Sweetheart
Says Hussein, she's the bride who dances
        despite the muddy feet

102

O Mother, who else would understand
my state since the separation? Smoke
rises out of the fire lit by the Master
Each time I poke I see red
Thorns drive me crazy
I obsess over the distance
The bread of sorrow, the curry of thorns,
now light up the stove of sobs
Forest and wilderness she searches
        Haven't found Lal yet
Once he meets me, I'll be joyful,
says Hussein, the wretched fakir

103

O Mother I'm going crazy. Look at the noisy world!
One carried on a palanquin, the other rides a horse
One cremated, the other buried. I have seen them
go barefoot, those with millions and billions
Here a king, there a pauper, here an ascetic, there a thief
Says Hussein, the lowly fakir, cattle are better than us

104

Your lover is mad at you, say my scornful girlfriends
Your indifference is my infamy, yet my gaze fixed on you

105

The lover gets sulky. I don't know what to do, folks
He's mine, I'm his, for his sake I'm on my way, folks
Help me meet my lover, folks, and I'll be your unpaid servant
Says Hussein, the Sain's fakir, the meeting is my fulfilment

Bad, bad, bad, we're bad, folks
Avoid us, the ill-reputed

Sharper than arrows and swords
the agony of separation, folks

Our lovers turned into travellers
We return after the farewells

If you are the Sain of Hazara
Then we the debutantes of Sial

Who'd care for the family or caste?
We set out in search of the lover, folks

Those who don't evoke the name of Sain
Later they'll be the regretful ones, folks

Says Hussein, the Sain's fakir, why worry?
We, the sinful, are the favourites of the Master

107

A place where God is not praised
is a place worth dogs and crows

Don't you know the essence of sandalwood
comes forth when scraped against a stone?

You joke around with common fools
You pull down the veil for the handsome

Says Hussein, the Sain's fakir, you are tipsy
on quite a few litres worth of swoon

108

Finally the meek had their day
Your pious white robe was hurled into fire
Better the tattered cloak of fakirs
At the shrine she's the bride who stood up
            for an unrestrained dance
Says Hussein, the Sain's fakir,
That's how you'll find refuge

109

Nothing else is accepted there
It's a matter of pure passion, Mister

One sits ash-smeared, gazing fixedly
The other roams the wild barefoot
Their hearts devoid of sincere longing

One stays up all night, praying
The other walks on coals, starves to death
Their place is not among the chosen

One reads the words of the Quran
The other engages in oral exegesis
It's not a matter of laughter and pride

Go to the door of the Perfect One
Beg the blessing for the beloved
Then you'll know the state of grace

Says Hussein, the beggar fakir,
the conclusion of a million sophistries:
the lover asks for the passion

110

Thieves carry out new thefts,
addicts constantly crave the drugs,
the busy bee worries about business
I need the remembrance of Sain

Kings rule their kingdoms, the rich
collect their loans, nobles run the estates
This one game my Sain started
I shall follow its strange rules

All plays I shall play before I get home
When people start to quarrel,
you help save my dignity, Sain
All die and settle in dust

One called Shah Hussein is a fakir,
        don't call him a master
I'm not fond of falsehood

111

Wasted your time in idle talk
Didn't make use of the opportunity
Slept with a sheet stretched over
You knew what was to be done
but no deed did you accomplish
You'll cry blood while giving the account
Go ask the wayfarers being driven by passion
who feared the overt expressions
Says Hussein what's to be told:
You'll regret once you reach the place
where you must go companionless

112

What did you do since you got here?
What will you say when you get there?

No wool you sheared, carded, or combed
What will you spin without a thread?

No loom you rolled, no yarn you spun
How do you expect the warp and weft?

No journey you planned, no luggage prepared
What will you carry in your trousseau?

Shah Hussein, I'm the dowry-less
Talk is cheap. No lover did I lure

113

Blessed are the paths along which came the beloved
Throw away the weaver's basket, I don't feel like
        spinning any more
A spark flew out of Heer's heart and Ranjha
        came down from Hazara
Says Hussein, the lowly fakir, God helped meet the Friend

114

Why would I be called a learned scholar?
Beg for bread, the kind of work I'll do
Sing my merry hymns, sitting right here at home
Passion is the fakir's walking stick, a strange fact
        beyond intelligence
Every moment I must focus on God
No other recitation except the name
of Sain, I must convince my heart
Lal, I am inside out, that's my business,
        that's my occupation
Together we shall dance the *jhurmat*

114 (A)

Spread your pack, dear fortune teller
Tell me when the Sweetheart arrives
The riverbanks turn verdant, the absence
blossoms all around, the branches bend
      lower, bearing my passion
Watch how I cover the distances, cross
the streams, walk past the lions asleep
No other purpose, no other longing
but wait out my days for the beloved
Again Shah Hussein cries out:
Sain! I yearn for your sight, turn
towards me for a single glance

115

I got stuck on the indifferent one,
the lord of the world and beyond
The mullah and scholar give advice
The wise and truthful show the path
Not straight and sorted are the ways of passion
Across the river dwells my Ranjha
I must fulfil what I promised
I plead before the boatman
Says Hussein, the wretched fakir,
death comes, the world's left behind
In the end we must deal with Allah

116

Tell, Mother, tell. Do tell the Sain my woes
Love threads my innards, thorns stitch my skin
Why give birth, naïve Mother, give life to sin?
Says Hussein, the wretched fakir, God knows better

117

Don't be proud, beauty and wealth will defraud you
Fooled by the swans I ended up with a gull

On a lotus leaf the water drops appear
as pearls. That's how you define the world

Cruelty, connivance, lies, intrigue fill our lives
Says Hussein, they got it, those who saw ahead

118

Congratulate me, you all, my pretty lover is home
The lover I was seeking high and low finally paid a visit
My courtyard glitters, my veranda sparkles, my face glows
Says Hussein, the lowly fakir, my Master led home
          the Friend

119

Indifferent Sain, my honour rests upon you
Four men lifted my bridal palanquin
dropped me at the groom's house
The spindle got stuck, the thread broke
Half-heartedly I spun the yarn
The crow took the rest
Dark night, muddy streets,
I ran into the night watchman. Says Hussein,
the lowly fakir, this is all I understood

120

I crave my Ranjha
I seek him high and low
He's right here with me
The cattle returned from the pastures,
my sweet herder didn't come, cries Heer in a grove
Day and night I wander through the thick forest, rocks
pierce my soles. Says Hussein, the wretched fakir,
      get Ranjha by any means necessary

121

O Girlfriend, I'm so tired of spinning
the cobwebbed cotton balls, I twiddle a pair of spools
The crow leaps at the single spindle I worked all day
I'm dressed up and the lover pays no attention
Either my luck ran out or my twisted fate
Good that the handloom broke, freeing my life
from drudgery. Says Hussein, the Sain's fakir,
I have seen the world meander towards the end

122

The Sain watches over dervishes and lovers
They don't distinguish between the revealed and hidden,
the difficult and easy, feast and sorrow. Delirious
they remain forever. Says Hussein: This is
the truth eternal and the rest all ephemeral

123

Watch out, Traveller, don't leave the luggage untended
No headdress or scarf safe here, this town full of thieves
You'll be regretful while arguing your case
Only then will you find all about this place
Water leaks from all sides, today or tomorrow
       your pot breaks
Says Hussein, the Sain's fakir, your life
       flows down into oblivion

124

The parents arranged my marriage,
didn't give much time to prepare
The in-laws here, I go without a trousseau
O mighty Lord, I had no clue
the ties being untied
Death severs brother and sister
Come, girlfriends, I'm about to be raised
upon the pallet for the bridal bath
No festivities later, this our only chance
Mother sobs inconsolably, sister stands weeping
Izrael, the angel, taking away the poor thing
Dark is the cell and no lamp left
The angel of death drags you by the arm,
no friend or companion. Leave behind
the self and arrogance, get hold of humility,
remember the wretched grave, your native land
Wring your hands or shake your head, but time
will deceive you. Says Hussein, the lowly fakir,
            friends must travel on

125

Have your fun out in the courtyard, but remember
they draw closer, those who recite Har's name often
Streams flow in the courtyard, flotillas float past
Deeds make you drown, deeds help swim across
Nine doors to this court, the tenth under lock
The one reserved for the lover is the door I know not
A nice niche in the courtyard, a box inside the niche
Inside the box I set the stage for a night with my beloved
In this courtyard an elephant swoons and pulls at the chain
Says Hussein, the wretched fakir, who would wake the wakened

126

You shall see the Lord, O Fakir, bend even lower
Your hat's dirty, not enough soap, sit by a riverbank scrubbing
The water buffalo is milked indoors, keep your devotion private
The streams gushed and flooded, I stood by the bank, steady
Says Hussein, the Sain's fakir, let happen what's got to happen

127

I cried out my lover's name so often
          I turned into Ranjha myself
Call me Ranjha, no one call me Heer
The beloved I was looking for, the beloved I found
Says Hussein, the company of dervishes allayed all doubts

~

Variation

The way you call, says the Sain,
is the way you shape the answer
Ranjha, I cried, Ranjha, I repeated
again and again till the syllables
of his name merged into mine
Ranjha I became and refused
          to answer
if anyone called me Heer

128

O my Sweetheart, the Saviour heard me
The world values the worldly, the sadhu prides in nudity
I'm laughed at since I'm neither bare to the skin
nor do I own anything worth this world
Love ignited the spark and the world
I left behind. A wanderer I became
Says Hussein, the Sain's fakir,
He knows better, the Omniscient

129

Don't waste your time turning the waterwheel at dusk
Go home with the beloved, avoid the frivolous quarrels
One filled up, one didn't fill, one thought it's too late
You'll regret it later, girl, once you're caught in a whirlpool
Says Hussein, the Sain's fakir, you won't be coming here again

130

Rise if you're asleep, time to please your lover
Two young men, on your right and left shoulder,
keep count of your good and bad
You won't get this moment again
You'll be miserable later. Says Hussein:
How will you answer when the lover takes account?

131

You'll regret it later, girl, go get your lover's favours
Red and green dresses—you're busy pleasing yourself
All your colours will fade if the lover is annoyed for a moment
Where are your mates? All buried beneath the barren ground
Where's your youthfulness? Where your sashaying beauty?
Where the speed and alacrity? Without the Sain a useless game
Where's your gold and silver, your pearls and gems?
          Into the dust
went your wealth. Look, there stands your wedding party
Says Hussein, the humble fakir, get going on the Sain's path

132

Don't turn your grace away even if I fall short
The true guru's cup of love I drank from and lost my senses
Setting aside the family and customs I go to my beloved
Says Hussein, the devotee of the Sain, your name is my fame

133

Girlfriends, help me meet my lover,
      I'm getting too restless
I won't ask the parents for dowry,
      won't ask for any valuables
Again and again I ask only for Ranjha
      to pull Heer out of her misery
They forced my marriage, dragged me
in circles around the wedding fire
I cried and screamed, they tied
my knot to the cruel Khera
I count the stars at night, the days
      I pass upon the thorns
I shall patiently serve my Ranjha
even if we rendezvous in dreams
Black the nights, black the cows
seeking the pastures to graze
Says Hussein, the wretched fakir,
may God unite the sundered

134

This is no place for words, my love
Inside and outside dwells the same Sain
To whom will you go tell? No other but
the same Sweetheart settled in all hearts
Says Hussein, the wretched fakir,
sacrifice yourself for the true guru

135

My arms around my lover's neck
How can I let him go? Like an addict's opium
he's settled in my bones. What's the joy of life
          without the constant evocation of Ram?
Says Hussein, the Sain's fakir, embrace the Master

136

O my Life, time for deeds is passing
Find yourself a corner, all night long
work your cloth. One wrong weave
may not go well with the Master
Short is life, long the remorse
Death won't spare whether a raja or a notable
Some new, some worn, some remain half-done
Says Hussein, the Sain's fakir, death needs no reason

137

I keep consoling the child
Brought the balm, didn't work; consulted the wise healers
Gone the dark, came the grey dawn, why cry over lost time?
To the mouth of five streams I went. Why blame the boatman?
Says Hussein, the Sain's fakir, why argue against the divine will?

~

Variation

I keep consoling this child-like heart. Consulted
the medicine men, bought the prescription
My malady can't be cured by syrups
My dark hair streaked grey
ferrying between the five streams
Why blame the poor boatman
merely following the course
ordained for wanderers?

138

One day you'll remember the hometown alleys
Bees flew off the flowers, leaves fell off the branches
I searched the wild, each plant I examined for the sign
One by one the weaver women called by the husbands
Their nights proved worth smouldering for the beloved
Only the inflamed knows the flame. The rest is idle chatter
Says Hussein, the Sain's fakir, your separation burns

139

It is sunny and bright as long as you're alive
No news of the dead beyond the dark
Four men lifted the bridal palanquin
Mother-in-law, sisters-in-law mocked:
          here comes the dowry-less
They carry out the will of the Mighty
Into a wretched grave I go, my wishes unfulfilled
Says Hussein, the miserable fakir, the world
must be left behind. So ordains the Almighty

Temporary is this stay, let's talk of taking off
Three and a half feet is the man's property
The wretched grave, the home
High mansion, glittering balconies, a fancy entrance
The wealth you're so proud is the den of enemies
Life's given, you come. God calls, you must go
Before the Master asks for the record, do something
Says Hussein, God's fakir, the world must be forsaken
      Die before dying

141

Won't return to the world again
Not forever the mustard blooms
Not forever rains the monsoon
Your prime lasts four days
why get caught up in lies?
Four days at the father's house
Then to the in-laws you must go
Shah Hussein, the Sain's fakir,
into the wilderness we settle

142

The one who cries can't sleep
The one who aches is the one who cries
No one sleeps well on a thorny bush
I'm all muddied, who'll wash and scrub?
Why call a doctor or a wise man?
You are the medicine for this pain
Says Hussein, the Sain's fakir,
only the ordained happens

143

Who do you think you are, Hussein?
Amid the jasmine and marwa
I, too, a blooming dandelion
False the world, false the pride
The puffed-up world struts around
Shah Hussein, get this into your head:
uproot arrogance, cultivate humility

144

Your head or your Sweetheart, choose
If you are a true connoisseur, spare
the empty boasts. Tempt with your red lips, go
up the gallows, swing. Truly, the silent ones walk
in the company of truth. Those who recognize
the truth, Shah Hussein, they understand
love in its completion. For them cometh
      the lover

~

Variation

Head or heart? Choose one
Dare the kiss, don't fear the gallows
If you aren't the type then spare the boast
The lover comes for those who evoke him
      in silence

145

Know thyself, Fellow
Easier to find God if you know
         who you are
Tall mansion, a bed of gold, consider it
a cremation ground if Har is not with you
No resident lasts here then why the arrogance?
         Says Hussein, God's fakir,
ephemeral is the universe, Fellow

146

Reflect on it for a moment: What's a heart?
Breath is the life source. The human was made
to meditate. And you got distracted by amusements
One thing in the heart and another on the lips
The world revolves. Shah Hussein, a wanderer,
watches life's caravans passing, passing

147

The whole world begs your favours, O Ram
I ask for an earthen pot, a wooden stick,
        a store of marijuana
Give me a sieve cloth, red pepper,
Don't make me plead for colour
Give me opium, a bowl, a basin full of sugar
Give me focus, awareness, a sadhu's company
Shah Hussein, the Sain's fakir, this
        a mendicant's prayer

~

Variation

You are the great giver, O Rama
Give me the paraphernalia
for bhang-making: a mortar 'n' pestle,
a sieve cloth, red pepper, plenty of sugar
Give my intoxicant the perfect colour and strength
Give me the companionship of a fellow outcast
Give me the ingredients of a fakir's contentment

148

For the sake of the friend, sieve the heart's blood
The liver I diced into pieces yet I don't deserve you

Nothing else left to serve except this bowl of water
No sleep I get lying on a bed, the cruel separation tortures

I could write and send you a book, but read
      the page of my heart
Painful nights, worrisome days, now the eyes as if
      pierced by lances

Do turn around sometime, take a look at this wretched girl
Do whatever you feel like, Sweetheart,
      strange is the path of passion

Days and night I think of you. Get me across
      any way you like
For your sake I roam freely, barefoot I search the forest

The eyes weep and plead: What did this wretched girl
      do wrong?

The sorrows severed me from all: I have no
        family, no in-laws

You are the last hope, grab hold of this naïve girl's sleeve

Says Hussein, the lowly fakir, unique are the ways
        of the downtrodden
This malady makes you stumble and stagger, but ahead
        lies the truth

149

I shattered my body and soul
and you take no pity, dear friend
Nothing else pleases or appeases
What else can the wretched do?
Says Hussein, the helpless fakir,
I won't accept anyone except you
You are the wisdom and the sight
You are the help for the helpless

150

Don't get entangled except for one entanglement
Tangle within a tangle often gets you strangled
Difficult terrain, tortuous paths, do you understand now?
Leave pride, adopt humility, you'll get there somehow
The flood lost its ferocity, the boatman rows away
Says Hussein, the wretched fakir, let the destined happen

151

O Hussein, the weaver! He earned no profit
Never got engaged, never got married
Never fixed a date, never held a wedding
Neither a householder nor a traveller
Neither a man of faith nor an infidel
       He is what he is

152

I found, I found, I found my beloved
He's settled in heaven, earth, water, air
Each thing encompassed, he said, *I was the hidden treasure*
Says Hussein, this the incantation taught by Shah Jalal

Notes and References

I. The Disgraceful Saint: An Introduction

1. Shafqat Tanvir Mirza, *Shah Hussain* (Islamabad: LokVirsa Publishing House, n.d.), retrieved from http://www.apnaorg.com/books/hussain/hussain.php?fldr=book.

2. Jahangir, *Tuzk-i-Jehangiri (Memoirs of the Emperor Jahangueir)*, trans. David Price (London: Oriental Translation Committee, 1829), retrieved from https://archive.org/details/memoirsofemperor00jaharich.

3. Shah Hussein, *Kafis: Shah Hussein*, ed. Muhammad Asif Khan (Lahore: Pakistan Punjabi Adabi Board, 2014; 6th edn), pp. 19–20.

4. Muhammad Pir, *Haqiqat al-Fuqra (Truth of the Saints)*, trans. (from Farsi to Urdu) Moulvi Syed Ahmed (Lahore: Panjnad Academy, 2007), p. 50. Translated from Urdu to English by Naveed Alam.

5. Noor Ahmed Chisti, *Tehqiqat-i-Chisti: Tarikh-i-Lahore ka Encyclopedia (Researches of Chisti: Encyclopedia of Lahore's History)* (Lahore: Al Faisal Nashran, 2006).

6. Ibid.

7. Ibid., pp. 60–61.

8. N. Hanif, *Biographical Encyclopaedia of Sufis (South Asia)*, (New Delhi: Sarup and Sons, 2000; 1st edn), p. 147.

9. Shah Hussein, *Poetry of Shah Hussein*, ed. Syed Nazir Ahmed (Lahore: Babar Ali Foundation, 2014; 3rd edn), p. 3.

10. Jean Genet, *Our Lady of the Flowers*, trans. Bernard Frechtman (New York: Grove Press, 1963), p. 126.

11. Annemarie Schimmel, *Mystical Dimensions of Islam* (North Carolina: University of North Carolina Press, 1978).

12. Najm Hosain Syed, *Recurrent Patterns in Punjabi Poetry* (Lahore: Farid Bhandar Trust, 2003), p. 21.

13. Ibid., p. 21.

14. W.H. Moreland, *From Akbar to Aurangzeb: A Study in Economic History* (London: Macmillan, 1923).

15. Najm Hosain Syed, *Takht L'hore (Throne of Lahore)* (Lahore: Rut Leykha, 2000).

16. Sultan Bahu, *Complete Abyat of Sultan Bahu*, ed. Muhammad Sharif Sabir (Fairfax, VA: Academy of Punjab in North America, n.d.), Bait 10, lines 2–4, retrieved from http://www.apnaorg.com/poetry/bahu/bahu5.html (translated by Naveed Alam).

17. Bulleh Shah, *Kalam Bulleh Shah* (Academy of Punjab in North America), retrieved from http://www.apnaorg.com/poetry/bullah/79.htm (translated by Naveed Alam).

18. Shah Hussein, *Kafis*, pp. 29–50.

19. Shah Hussein, *Kafis*.

20. Madho Lal Hussein, *Kafis of Madho Lal Hussein*, ed. Najm Hosain Syed (Lahore: Suchet Kitab Ghar, 2014).

21. Shah Hussein, *Maiy Ni Mein Kino Akhan (O Mother To Whom Can I Tell): Poetry of Shah Hussein*, ed. and trans.

(from Punjabi to Urdu) Saleem Akhtar (Lahore: Book Home, 2010).

II. Kafis

The number before the dot corresponds with the number of the kafi in the text; the number following the decimal indicates the line.

1. The numbering of the kafis is not based on any authenticated preference of the poet. I am following the order of the APNA website: http://www.apnaorg.com/poetry/shah/shfront.html. Almost the same order is followed in most texts including the ones compiled by Muhammad Asif Khan (*Kafis of Shah Hussein*), Najm Hosain Syed (*Kafis of Madho Lal Hussein*) and Saleem Akhtar (*Maiy Ni Mein Kino Akhan* (*O Mother To Whom Can I Tell*): *Poetry of Shah Hussein*).

1.3. *Tana bana* (warp and weft), two key words, signify: (a) the intensity of union with the beloved through the loss of individual self (as opposed to the lover being the warp and the beloved being the weft), and (b) the weaver's diction commonly used throughout Hussein's oeuvre.

1.4. In Arabic, fakir means poor, but in Punjabi, it's the mendicant, dervish, beggar, pauper. What kind of a fakir is Hussein? He is a *fakir nimana*—a fakir without *ma'an* or pride, worthless, wretched, of the lowest order, a lumpen proletariat. But remember, *Shah Hussein's humility cuts like an axe* (kafi 34), for he's a *malamati*, blameworthy, an outcast, a rebel, a transgressor of the bogus conventions of love, the one who breaks free.

2.1. Shah Hussein is known to wander around in a red dress. Madho will also be addressed as 'Lal' in kafi 21.

2.4. 'Don't translate Sain [pronounced *Sai'n*] into "lord",' Najm Hosain Syed advised me. He didn't know how the plain-spoken kafis reminded me of the earthy American blues and gospel music. *Oh Lord, have mercy. Lordy Lord, hang low the sweet chariot. Lawd, I ain't getting drunk no more.* But I couldn't ignore what he was pointing at: the reality of the Indo-Pak subcontinent where the dark native often resorted to the most menial and unctuous terms to ingratiate himself with the white colonizer, the lord and master. Lord fails to convey what Sain evokes: the guardian, saviour, watcher, protector, the companion who comes to the succour of the despairing. Might as well let the reader enjoy the sound of Sain the way I savoured the syllables while memorizing the various names of Shiva when I first came across the poetry of Dhurjati and Mahadeviyakka: Srikalahasti, Cennamulkarjuna, Kundalasangamadeviya.

2. Variations, looser translations that accompany some of the kafis, are exercises in interpretive exploration. This particular variation attempts to bridge the sensual and spiritual elements within the folkloric theme of spinning.

3.1. A Punjabi group dance.

3.4. A play on the word *khuddi*, literally a hole, but also the space a weaver places his feet in while working on the warp of the cloth.

4.5. Reference to the garb of the scholar or noble.

5.8. The narrator is sleeping on a *choubara*, a common feature of Indo-Pak architecture—a shed-like structure above the highest floor with entrances and windows on all four sides. A well-ventilated space offering privacy.

7.1. Hussein rarely uses Allah. If not Sain, then it is Rab, Maula, Ram. Actually, he uses Ram quite often (see kafis 68, 80, 81, 89). He even evokes Har, Shiva (kafis 125, 145). Perhaps perceived as the god of nobles, sultans and emperors, Allah was not in vogue among the common folk Hussein chose to associate with.

10. The variation came about after listening to this kafi being sung by G. Hussein Baksh (http://www.apnaorg.com/poetry/shah/shah5.html). For a queer interpretive version, see the translator's poem, *Message*, published in the online journal *The Adirondack Review* (http://www.theadirondackreview.com/shahhussein.html).

11.5. Sheikh, the scholar, is also the family name of Hussein. The brunt of this line turns inwardly into self-rebuke.

15.5. Added to the anti-intellectualism is the note of anti-establishment. According to Muhammad Pir's *Haqiqat al-Fuqra*, when Emperor Akbar asked Hussein for any wish to be granted, Hussein requested he never be summoned to the royal court again.

15.7. The Islamic angel of death.

21.1. The only kafi where Madho Lal is addressed directly, though 'Lal' can also be interpreted as the general term of endearment. Also see kafis 101, 114.

23. One of those kafis that can easily go both ways: supplication to the human as well as the divine beloved.

25.3. The disgrace here for proximity to the lover lends itself to the queer interpretation. In pursuit of Madho, Hussein moved across the river Ravi to the town of Shahdara. The two later cohabited together.

29. One of the most elusive kafis—if it could be called a kafi, since it does not conform to the typical stanzaic form. The red wedding dress, references to the various places of the Indian subcontinent (Kashmir, Gujarat, Multan) and then the image of Krishna with his flute—all add to the mystery. The consistent rhyming pattern (the last word of each line rhymes) propels it forward and suggests the performative aspect, perhaps an adaptation of the wedding song to the situation of the narrator, a bride with an uncertain or indifferent groom.

32.5. The literal translation of 'reaping regrets' would be 'regrets at the end or resultant regrets'. During a *Sangat* session, Najm Hosain Syed offered the following meanings for the Punjabi word *an't*: end, result, goal, agenda, target. The translator's choice of 'reaping' tries to preserve the poetic integrity by drawing a link with the agrarian imagery of the second line, the blooming mustard fields.

37.7. Mansoor al-Hallaj (c. 858–922), a Persian mystic and poet who cried out *an'al haq* (I am the Truth). Orthodox scholars and jurists accused Mansoor of blasphemy saying only Allah is the Truth. Mansoor was convicted after a lengthy trial and executed. The Sufis often invoke him as a symbol of ecstatic union between the divine lover and the mortal beloved, a state that liberates the daring lover from the fear of death.

42.10. In this line, there's a reference to the specific part of the loom called *bai'r*, a thin rope that joins the spokes of the double wheels. It's covered with a sturdier rope and aids the circular motion making a *to'n* (means *you* in Punjabi) sound. The loom as a whole makes the sound of *sain sain*. The whole contraption of the loom is referred to as a device that constantly pays homage to the Master (You are the Sain, you are the Sain), a prayer wheel of sorts.

43.12. Death before dying, a common refrain in the Sufi poetry. It signifies the importance of killing the selfish ego for the sake of attaining selflessness and thus qualifying for the beloved. Jamal Elias chose it as the title for his translations of Sultan Bahu's poetry which was published by the University of California Press. Also see kafis 53, 94.

43.16. In one of the earlier versions I translated this line as: 'The body of the beloved is the doorway to God.' I curbed my interpretive instinct heeding Anne Carson, the translator of Sappho: '[T]he more I stand out of the way, the more Sappho shows through. This is an amiable fantasy (transparency of self) within which most translators labour.' See Anne Carson, 'Introduction,' in *If Not, Winter: Fragments of Sappho* (New York: Vintage Books, 2002), p. X.

45. This kafi is not in Punjabi but Persianized Hindi, similar to the *brij bhasha* of Amir Khusrau. Also see kafi 90.

55.2. As a patriarchal norm, a bride leaves the parents' house (*paykay*) to join the husband's family (*susral*). In this line, there's a reference to the particular custom (*muklawa*) of the bride returning to her *susral* after a short sojourn at her *paykay*. Literal translation: 'Today or tomorrow is *muklawa*.'

56.8. The figure of five is often symbolic of the five senses in Sufi poetry. The senses lead us astray, perpetuate the illusion, dissuade us, carry us away from the truth. Note the five spindles the ingénue carries in her weaving basket in the upcoming kafi 60. Kafi 79 further corroborates this idea.

56.8. Plural of *kaseera*, a coin lesser in value than a paisa. Picayune.

58.2. Bhang is a cheap intoxicant made with crushed marijuana leaves and milk. It's still readily available at many of the Sufi shrines, especially during the festive anniversaries. *Bhangi*, a bhang drinker, is also a term used for sweepers or janitors.

61.3. Another five. Hussein does not exactly say five 'senses', but the assumption is being made based on the preceding kafis and general Sufi philosophy. Literal translation of the first two lines: 'Round and round turn the wheel, O Woman, and keep it turning / Why regret the five, Vagabond? One can get the fame.'

63. *Changi aan kay mandi aan/ mein sahib teri bandi aan*—one of the signature songs of Abida Parveen, the famous Pakistani singer of mystical poetry.

69.10. A chess-like game. The two lines sound like the fragment of a ditty.

72. Variation. As Pathanay Khan, a kafi virtuoso, sings, he pauses, stretches and repeats certain lines lending a unique melancholic cadence to the poetry. Besides the interpretive approach, the use of tercets in this variation is an attempt to reflect the flow as well as the fugue-like structure of the singer's rendition.

73.4. Heer's family hastily arranged her marriage with a member of the Khera family, their social equals, to prevent the ignominy of her affair with Ranjha, a servant.

73.6. Ranjha served Heer's household as a cattle herder to stay close to Heer.

80.3. *Jind*, the word for life, has been used as *jindo*, an affectionate way to address someone younger in age—like the Spanish word for a fat person (*gorda*) sometimes becomes *gordito*.

80.7. The in-laws, the *muklawa* givers. For *muklawa*, see kafi 55.

81.8. 'Khan of Khans' or *Khan-e-Khana* was the title of Khanzada Mirza Khan, popularly known as Abdul Rahim Khan-e-Khana, one of the nine important ministers (*navaratna*s or nine gems) of Akbar's court. He was also a poet who signed off his poems as Rahim. According to some hagiographers, Hussein gave the blessing of a military victory to Khan-e-Khana when he came as a supplicant to the saint; however, this kafi points out something different: a caveat of mortality to the powerful. See also kafi 83.

81.9. *Kal*—a possible reference to Kali.

89.1. A form of dance.

90. Kafi in *brij bhasha*. See kafi 45.

90.2. The game was brought to the subcontinent by the Central Asian armies. Sultan Qutub-uddin Aibak, known for the famous Qutb Minar, died playing polo in Lahore in AD 1210.

95 (A). This kafi is part of kafi 95 in the online text posted on the APNA (Academy of the Punjab in North America) website, but separated in Muhammad Asif Khan's text. Due to the shift in the rhyming pattern, I am also treating it as a separate kafi.

99.7. Perhaps the loudest and clearest message to the hagiographers who succeeded in canonizing Hussein. Also see the conclusion of kafi 110.

102.1. Arguably the most popular kafi. Literal translation of the first two lines: 'O Mother, to whom can I tell / the state of separation's ache?' The choice of my phrasing hints at why the mother is the ideal figure to empathize since she herself has suffered the pangs of primal separation: the child being taken out of her womb. The child becomes conscious of such a separation later, much later, perhaps in a different context, through a different experience.

102.4. Here, *Lal* could mean the colour red, beloved, or Madho Lal. Also see the following note.

102.10. The only kafi with two references to Lal.

106.7. Reference to Ranjha who came from the city of Takht Hazara.

106.8. Reference to Heer who belonged to Sial.

114.9. Madho Lal or the colour red? I'd prefer the former.

114.11. A Punjabi group dance with orchestrated movements danced in a circle.

114 (A). Kafi 114 and 114 (A) are treated as a single kafi in the online text; however, it's been separated in the text edited by Muhammad Asif Khan. I have chosen to follow the latter text because of the sudden shift in theme and tone despite the same rhyming scheme.

115.11. One of the rare mentions of Allah. Mostly Sain, Ram, Rab and Maula have been used. See kafi 116.

117.6. The last phrase is based on Muhammad Asif Khan's version. The online version (those who *recognized the Rab*) breaks the preceding rhyming pattern.

124.3. See the notes for kafis 55 and 80.

125. A riddle-like kafi. Ten doors, a niche, a box, a bridal stage inside the box, and finally a dwarf elephant add to the esoteric aspects of this kafi.

130.2. According to Muslims, two angels, Munkar and Nakeer, sit on the right and left shoulder respectively of every human, keeping account of the sins and good deeds. On the Day of Judgment, the fate of every individual will be decided on the written account presented by the duo.

134. According to some sources, Shah Hussein travelled to Amritsar to get his poetry included in the Granth Sahib being compiled by Guru Arjun Dev (1563–1605). He offered this kafi for inclusion. Though the account is unverifiable, the thematic content of this kafi might have lent itself to the speculation.

135. The first line of this kafi is the same as that of kafi 13 except for a change of word (*hand* has been replaced by *neck*).

According to many editors of Shah Hussein's poetry, Dr Mohan Singh Diwana found a handwritten Gurmukhi manuscript of twenty-five kafis in the Punjab University library (manuscript #374) which dated back to 1804, the oldest textual record of Hussein's work (see Shah Hussein, *Kafis*, pp. 13–14). This kafi as well as the following kafis with repetitive content are from the Punjab University manuscript. Dr Nazir Ahmed, one of editors of Hussein's work, claims to have found a total of forty-eight kafis in the same manuscript; however, seven of them were repeated, which leaves forty-one kafis.

138. Compare with kafi 9.

140. Compare with kafi 53.

141. Compare with kafi 32.

143. Compare with kafi 37. This kafi rhymes beautifully throughout (*mooli, gandhooli, phooli, samjholi* being the end words). Since the rhyming scheme is not followed in the translation, a phrase from the last line (let go of arrogance, get hold of humility) is translated in a manner (uproot arrogance, cultivate humility) so as to unify the floral imagery.

151. This kafi and kafi 152, according to Muhammad Asif Khan, are not from the Punjab University manuscript, but mentioned in Dr Mohan Singh Diwana's *A Brief History of Punjabi Literature* (p. 80). See Shah Hussein, *Kafis*, p. 213. Also see Shah Hussein, *Poetry of Shah Hussein*, p. 7.

152.3. The italicized phrases are in Arabic (*kullu sheyan mahit, kuntu kinzan*). The Quranic attributes of Allah.